Your Favorite Authors

GRACE LIN

by Abby Colich

CAPSTONE PRESS
a capstone imprint

First Facts are published by Capstone Press,
1710 Roe Crest Drive, North Mankato, Minnesota 56003
www.capstonepub.com

Library of Congress Cataloging-in-Publication Data
Colich, Abby.
 Grace Lin / by Abby Colich.
  pages cm.—(First Facts. Your Favorite Authors)
 Includes bibliographical references and index.
 Summary: "Presents the life and career of Grace Lin, including her childhood, education, and
milestones as a best-selling children's author"—Provided by publisher.
 ISBN 978-1-4765-3158-8 (library binding)
 ISBN 978-1-4765-3445-9 (paperback)
 ISBN 978-1-4765-3435-0 (eBook PDF)
1. Lin, Grace—Juvenile literature. 2. Authors, American—20th century—Biography—Juvenile
literature. 3. Illustrators—Biography—Juvenile literature. 4. Children's stories—Authorship—
Juvenile literature. I. Title.
 PS3562.I46774Z56 2014
 813'.6—dc23
 [B]   2013003118

Editorial Credits
Christopher L. Harbo, editor; Tracy Davies McCabe and Gene Bentdahl, designers;
Marcie Spence, media researcher; Kathy McColley, production specialist

Photo Credits
Capstone: Michael Byers, cover, 15 (bottom); Courtesy of Grace Lin: Alexandre Ferron, 5, 7,
9, 13, 15 (top), 16, 19, 21; Newscom: Andre Jenny, 11; Shutterstock: alex.makarova, design
element, Havlin Levente, design element, ImagePlus, design element, Jeffrey Lia, 17, Vivian
Liu, design element

Printed in the United States of America in North Mankato, Minnesota.
032013   007223CGF13

Table of Contents

Chapter 1: A Cinderella Night

Grace Lin got an exciting phone call in January 2010. Her book *Where the Mountain Meets the Moon* had won a Newbery Honor. This award is given to just a few of the best children's books every year. Lin was honored at a **banquet** in June. She called it her "Cinderella night."

---

banquet—a formal meal for a large number of people, usually on a special occasion

Lin (left) at the
Newbery banquet

WHERE THE MOUNTAIN
MEETS THE MOON

Grace Lin

Chapter 2:
Growing Up Asian-American

Grace Lin was born May 17, 1974, in New Hartford, New York. Her parents were **immigrants** from Taiwan. Grace had one older sister and one younger sister. The Lins were the only Asian family in the area. Grace wanted to fit in with everyone else. She tried to forget that she was Asian.

---

immigrant—a person who leaves one country and settles in another

Chinese Fairy Tales

Knowing Grace loved to read, her mom sneaked Chinese fairy tales onto Grace's bookshelf. She wanted Grace to learn about their **heritage**. During a trip to Asia many years later, Grace remembered the fairy tales. This experience helped inspire *Where the Mountain Meets the Moon.*

---

heritage—history and traditions handed down from the past

Grace wanted to be an ice skater when she grew up. But in the sixth grade, she entered a national writing contest for kids. Grace created a book about talking flowers called *Dandelion Stories*. She won fourth place and $1,000. From then on, Grace knew she wanted to be a book writer and **illustrator**.

---

illustrator—someone who draws pictures for books, magazines, or other publications

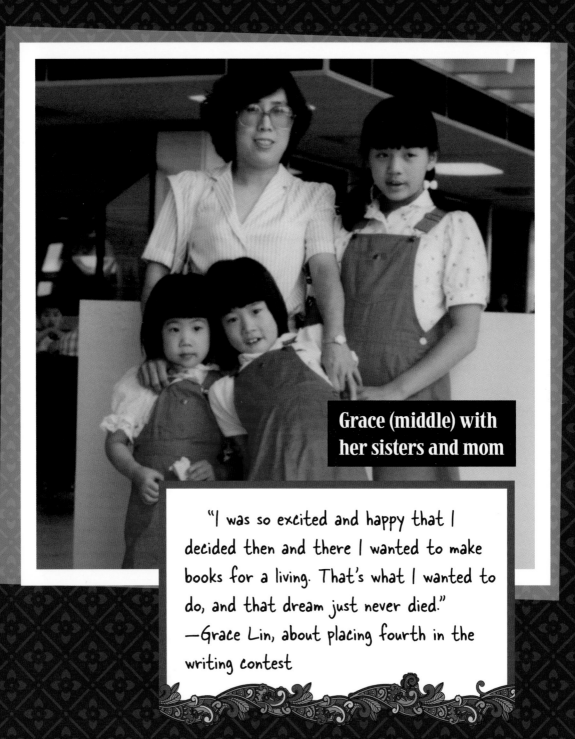

Grace (middle) with her sisters and mom

"I was so excited and happy that I decided then and there I wanted to make books for a living. That's what I wanted to do, and that dream just never died."
—Grace Lin, about placing fourth in the writing contest

Grace studied illustration at the Rhode Island School of Design. After she **graduated** in 1996, she tried to become a book illustrator. But she ended up working at a company that made mugs and T-shirts. Grace eventually lost that job. She tried again to go after her dream. She sent thousands of her illustrations to book **publishers**. But she never heard anything back.

---

graduate—to finish a course of study in school and receive a diploma

publisher—someone who makes and sells printed things such as newspapers or books

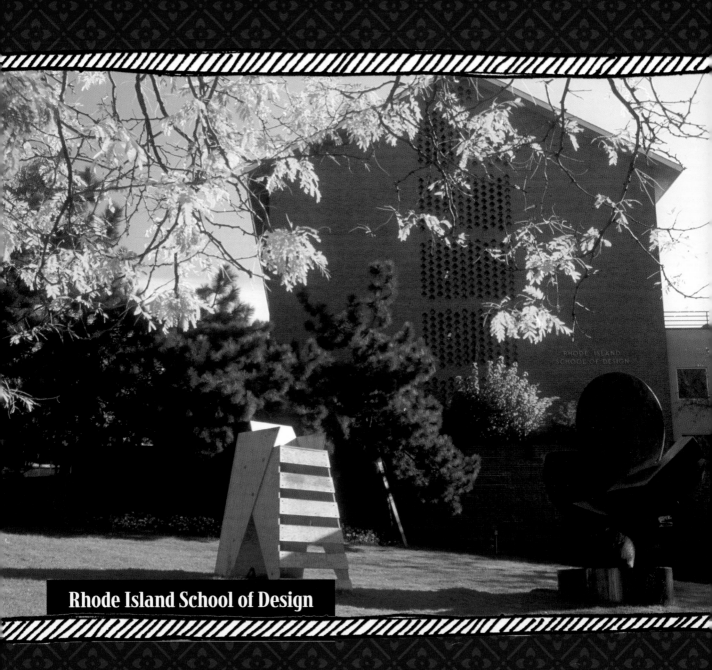

Rhode Island School of Design

Chapter 3:
Becoming a Writer and Illustrator

One day an **editor** finally told Lin that he liked her illustrations. He asked if she had a story to go with them. Lin fibbed and said that she did. She had to write fast to get the text finished. In 1999 her first book, *The Ugly Vegetables*, was published.

---

editor—someone who checks the content of a book and gets it ready to be published

Lin's dream of becoming a writer and illustrator was finally coming true. She worked hard to create more picture books. These included *Dim Sum for Everyone!, Okie-Dokie, Artichokie!,* and *Fortune Cookie Fortunes.* Many of Lin's books are about Asian culture and growing up as an Asian-American.

"... when I was younger I was uninterested in my Asian heritage. Writing about Asian culture is kind of my way of trying to get it back."—Grace Lin

The Year of the Dog was Lin's first **novel** for kids. It was published in 2006. The main character, Pacy, is based on Lin. Pacy was Lin's nickname growing up. Lin later wrote two more Pacy books. *The Year of the Rat* came out in 2008. *Dumpling Days* hit bookstores in 2012.

---

novel—a book that tells a long story about made-up people and events

Fact and Fiction

The Pacy books are fiction. But they are based on people and events from Grace Lin's childhood. For example, Lin went to Taiwan with her family like in *Dumpling Days*. But the part about visiting the Taipei 101 skyscraper is fiction. The tower was built after Lin's trip.

Taipei 101

In 2007 Lin began writing her first **fantasy** book. Then her husband, Robert, died from cancer. Lin did not think she could finish the book. But a friend convinced her to keep writing. *Where the Mountain Meets the Moon* received many honors and became a best-seller. Lin's second fantasy book, *Starry River of the Sky*, was published in 2012.

---

fantasy—a story set in an unreal world

Lin working in her studio

Chapter 4: Continuing Her Dream

Grace Lin thinks it is important to keep writing about Asian culture. She works hard in her studio writing, illustrating, and updating her blog. Each year she visits many schools. She reads from her books and does "draw-alongs." She lives with her husband, Alex, and their daughter in Massachusetts.

"The best thing that I always say to kids is, 'If you want to be a writer, you have to be a reader.' And that's very, very important ... I think you need to read books, and you need to love books."—Grace Lin

Timeline

1974	born May 17 in New Hartford, New York
1996	graduates from the Rhode Island School of Design
1999	first book, *The Ugly Vegetables*, is published
2001	marries her first husband, Robert; *Dim Sum for Everyone!* is published
2003	*Okie-Dokie, Artichokie!* is published
2004	*Fortune Cookie Fortunes* is published
2006	*The Year of the Dog* is published
2007	husband, Robert, dies from cancer
2008	*The Year of the Rat* is published
2009	*Where the Mountain Meets the Moon* is published
2010	*Where the Mountain Meets the Moon* wins the Newbery Honor; marries her husband, Alex
2012	*Dumpling Days* is published; daughter is born; *Starry River of the Sky* is published
2013	creates the official 2013 Children's Book Week bookmark

Glossary

banquet (BANG-kwit)—a formal meal for a large number of people, usually on a special occasion

editor (ED-uh-tur)—someone who checks the content of a book and gets it ready to be published

fantasy (FAN-tuh-see)—a story set in an unreal world

graduate (GRAJ-oo-ate)—to finish a course of study in school and receive a diploma

heritage (HER-uh-tij)—history and traditions handed down from the past

illustrator (IL-uh-strate-ur)—someone who draws pictures for books, magazines, or other publications

immigrant (IM-uh-gruhnt)—a person who leaves one country and settles in another

novel (NOV-uhl)—a book that tells a long story about made-up people and events

publisher (PUHB-lish-er)—someone who makes and sells printed things such as newspapers or books

Read More

Fandel, Jennifer. *You Can Write Awesome Stories*. You Can Write. North Mankato, Minn.: Capstone Press, 2012.

Llanas, Sheila Griffin. *Picture Yourself Writing Fiction: Using Photos to Inspire Writing*. See It, Write It. Mankato, Minn.: Capstone Press, 2012.

Index

Internet Sites

FactHound offers a safe, fun way to find Internet sites related to this book. All of the sites on FactHound have been researched by our staff.

Here's all you do:

Visit *www.facthound.com*

Type in this code: 9781476531588

Super-cool stuff!

Check out projects, games and lots more at
www.capstonekids.com